We have published Lorrie Ness more times than any poet in the history of our journal, and her new collection of poetry, *Anatomy of a Wound*, is testament to why. Intensely personal, yet effortlessly accessible, every poem is a luminous and unflinching journey through challenging human landscapes. Her svelte verse, elegant craft, and vivid imagery are constant companions throughout this tight collection. Ness's work is emotionally visceral and intellectually explosive. Few poets can transport readers the way Lorrie Ness can, and *Anatomy of a Wound* rewards them in beautifully unexpected ways that linger long after its words have left their lips.

—*Sky Island Journal*

Small, seamlessly textured and *mighty*. Lorrie Ness' *Anatomy of a Wound* rivets the reader to the tale of a mother's suicide and its pummeling effect on those close at hand. The leaps of imagery are color-infused, indelible to the memory and shaking. Her uses of metaphor are masterfully composed and always pitch-perfect. Rather than holding her characters at a distance like other, less- assured poets—Ms. Ness embraces them, albeit tentatively, more often than not. Here, relationships are both loving and horrifying as a mother's touch. I finished reading feeling rubbed raw—and alive.

—Robert Nazarene, founding editor,
The American Journal of Poetry

The poems here don't flinch. A mother's death by suicide is part of what this collection examines, yet Ness retains a fearless, critical eye throughout. Ness leaves no thread unexamined, teasing out each one without ever cutting it away from its place in the whole. The suicide itself is denied the power to drive this exploration. The poet remains, with rare and intentional exceptions, in charge. This control is masterful. The language is riveting, unafraid of the grittier truths of biology. This collection is a powerful debut.

—Jessica Federle

Lorrie Ness is a poet unafraid of biology. She is equally unafraid of beauty. In her opening words, it's declared "the body was out' - and undoubtedly, in this collection, it is. Blood, vomit, sweat, saliva, semen... name any kind of bodily excretion and it's bound to make an appearance in her work. Unflinchingly she guides us through the stink and smack of our bodies, their pain; there is little to no breathing room in this ruthless interrogation of the body. The reader is dared time and again to look away. What is remarkable is how she refuses in this viscerality to reduce a body to its biology or in dissecting it, extract its history and the love implicit in its cells. In this collection, the small intestine is adjacent to love is adjacent to loss, all of it coalescing into a dangerously tender and vital offering. Just as ruthlessly she pulls apart emotions and asks us to examine them in turn... In prying apart words and reassembling them, this collection is an autopsy in every sense of the definition. I read these poems unable to look away and this ultimately is what her work demands: the respect of eye contact. It's among the rarest, realest and bravest collections of poetry, from a formidable new voice.

—Andy Palanzuelo

In 'unskinned' language, Lorrie Ness' poignant poems remind us our stories/histories are natural elements, root balls of raw nerves we can move and replant elsewhere, in new soil. Ness' visions in vein blue and pale green inhabit writer's groups, gas station bathrooms, autopsies and hospitals, yet faded flowers continue to bloom out of season. Family, here, is the cost of living and not living, but our memories like our DNA, Ness seems to say, are the armature of our presence. Ultimately, these poems of spade and scalpel are complex and beautiful eulogies to our hands.

—Mark Waldron

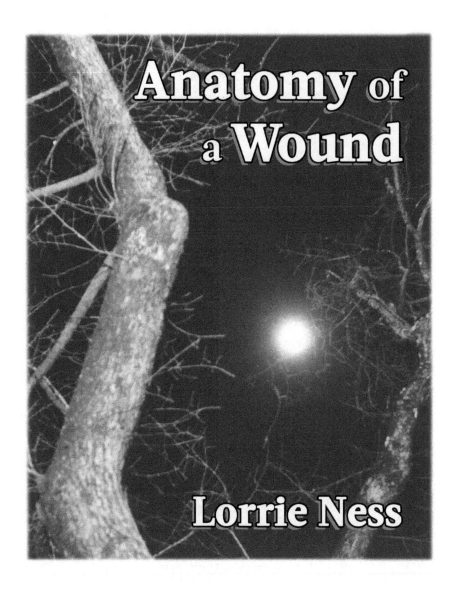

Anatomy of
a Wound

Lorrie Ness

Flowstone Press
Illinois Valley, Oregon

First Flowstone Press Edition • July 2021
ISBN 978-1-945824-48-7

Flowstone Press,
an Imprint of Left Fork

www.leftforkbooks.com

For my mother,
who set my life in motion.

For my grandmother,
who carried the torch when she was gone.

And for my husband and friends
who surround me.

Contents

Anatomy of a Wound

Unzipped

The body was out.
Cranium rocking on a steel cart. Brain
1308 grams. Stomach contents
thin, beige liquid. Samples taken
for lab analysis. Lead wadcutter bullet
lodged inside her vertebrae. Muzzle abrasion
2cm left of the umbilicus. Vena cava
severed, spinal cord too. I'm sure
there were fingers, skinned
in blue, nitrile gloves. Someone
held the softness of her right kidney. Someone
wrote it was surrounded by coagulation.
Surrounded. Like a defense? Like a siege?
Maybe both. The medical examiner
catalogued her organs, scraped her nails.
There is no mention of the saw,
the smell of burning hair and bone.
No details about the medical waste. A visor,
the plastic shoe covers flecked with my mother.
The report works its way to her facade.
203 pounds. Hair: brown. Collected
in a ponytail. Strands retained.
Pierced lobes, no tattoos.
Extensive liver mortice evident on ventral surfaces.
Hands bagged at the scene.
Swabbed for powder. Tox screen NEG.
Time of death, 11:11. Manner,
suicide.

Rewind

the first time i saw a baby bird
    i recognized my aunt sheila.

blue-veined & frail —all mouth
    below bulging eyes,

bones & innards
    rising beneath her skin. thinness

compressed her body into braille.
    at the pool she read herself by touch

& drank diet coke
    inside a fairy ring of bottles.

she made her own perimeters,
    edging the deep end

like a synonym for caution. her body
    sweated steadily into sky.

mom's shadow gave her shade. plump
    & demanding distance.

within a family without boundaries
    fat & bones were twins,

antonyms that meant unfuckable.
    each woman grew a shell,

an escape they could never outrun.
    their mother traded her father

for a brood. she nursed
    till her milk was silty with her dregs,

mining herself
    until the shaft hit mantle.

afterward, grandma spoke lava & pissed
    whiskey from her tongue,

pickling every man she mouthed,
    so we'd know them by smell.

in great-grandpa's wake, tobacco steeped the air.
    he wore tweed & coaxed

with a sleeve of fig newtons. he flashed
    yellow teeth. when i sat on his lap,

mother yanked me away so hard
    i was bruised as a bitten apple.

The Cost of Our First House

(great)grandpa rides the back-
hoe, oversees the footer.
he is the foreman making her
a house. he marked
mother with touch
& now he tells shirtless men
how deep she needs it,
leaves others to do the boring.

mother is newly married
& lately lost. looking at blueprints —
dotted lines tethering windows to switches,
doorways to ducts.
dotted lines are perforations
showing where to rip. she fingers the buttons
closing her shirt. longing
to feel square,

she presses herself
between roughed-in studs,
molds her flesh to an edge.
he marked mother with touch & now
she's been given to another man. (great)-
grandpa builds her walls. rooms
where narrow closets clamp
tightly to what they stow.

The Move

The weedy paths between the trailers
brimmed with castoffs.

Every household donated to the supply
of feral children and broken bottles.

Nikki the dirt urchin pedaled
like she could peel sunset off the road.

She was a fishtail of sand and the clatter
of rusty fenders coasting.

At dusk, mom would sit on the stoop listening
to her tires churning gravel.

We were new to Florida, living with dad's parents
in a mobile home edging an unpaved road.

There was no AC, just aluminum roofing
sealing in the summer heat.

Sweat from four adults and one child
marinated inside the walls.

Most evenings I came outside with mom
airing my legs in cutoffs as Nikki streaked by.

Lap after lap. Orbiting
like she was caught by the gravity of this place.

Nightfall was our renewable resource,
its shadows filling in the gaps of her ripped clothes,

transforming her briefly
before the sunrise tore her up once more.

She'd wait for her folks' light to go out,
then lean her bike against the chain link, tiptoe in.

Every evening it was the three of us
keeping vigil under the moon.

She Said It

i

Mine ain't an [every]body.
I'm more than two of you and that makes me less.

Every day he comes home to
blubbering-bitch and fat-fuck me raw. It's true,

mine's a body built for blame.

ii

You know why your dad pissed by the fence row
for a week every month?

He said it's because I was shameless —
throwing Tampax wrappers in the wastebasket.

Now I never stop. Bleeding
like a slaughtered hog.

iii

I can actually hear clots dripping
lip to bowl. He can't tell me this is just
female problems.

Listen to him bang at the door
calling *me* Jesus Christ.

If that were true,
he'd mine this trashcan for relics. Toilet paper
stained like my own Shroud of Turin.

Genesis

Every without carries weight.
Without a car. Without money.
Without insurance.
The mass began to grow.

Countdown

Mom bled three weeks.
    Then five weeks.
        After that we counted in months.

Leesburg Regional Medical Center
    Waterman Hospital
        UF Shands

Two days.
    Then four days
        after swallowing the hormone pills.

        Clots. Thrombosis.
    Pulmonary embolism. Gasping.
Exhale. Gasping. Exhale
Gasping.

        One year.
    Then two years.
After that there were only weeks.

She Spoke with Urgency

we construct our histories   with words
vaguely wet upwellings   of the throat
if each voice   is a maker's mark
mom's was the sound   of chestnuts steaming
meat hissing   inside their shells

she asked to talk   so that I would listen
pressing my ear   over a tender seam
released her pressure   left my lobe
scalding pink   she told me what's swallowed
no longer burns   inside the belly

language is unskinned   once it is spoken
leaving the mouth   raw and blistered
she closed her lids   shutting off their valves
to give her voice full volume   fearing her eyes
would syphon away   stories meant for her lips

Botany: A Side Effect of Treatment

throat sieves liquid
through snarled plumbing

remains of water engorge her toes —
oak buds purpled with spring

swollen & sweat-dropped —
body near full bloom

        ripe as the plums
        yielding to my knife

        peels splitting
        from a season of rain

        flesh dribbles & swells
        draws flies with its juice

        odor cankers the skin —
        her bouquet

mouth hydraulic
swallows while the body drowns

ulcers stoma her legs
bilge into sheets

knotted veins tangle her shins
like vines cultivated from bed

botanical name: phlebitis

thirst drove her to botany
a side effect of the pills & Florida heat

begging water while roots rot
i press slices of plums to her lips

peel away her soaking cotton
i cannot forget the smell

Voice Rise

A mother's tongue
is language rounded by water —
grammared by bone

I first knew her liquid form. Sloshing
in womb-black darkness.
Her voice was a ripple,
conducted mouthwarm and muffled,
down her spine to my blue-brined skin.

An impressionism of speech
like faces through frosted glass. Movement,
color and deckled edge.

Now her teeth glide along her words
like whetstones.

Softness and murmur have gone.

I curl a pillow around my ear,
translate her speech to the language I know.

Metamorphosis

I found you dozing in room 2132.
Swaddled in a chrysalis of blankets.

Legs so swollen,
your compression socks looked like pythons
swallowing salami.

I can hardly reconcile
our phone call.

How your mouth was wrapped around your voice
like an amphitheater. Broadcasting
volume and health.

And now you are empty. As if through talking,
you pressed the accelerator, chasing hits of energy
till your body shuddered
and came to a stop.

Today the nurses have wrapped you in a cocoon,
sky blue as the day we moved.
I think about that day —

As I watch you pupate inside your bundle,
it reminds me how our sleeping bags were a row of caterpillars
on the bare floor.

How your body begs again for the touch
of fleece.

Goodbye

The facts are simple.

She came into my room that February morning,
flipped the lights and smiled,
backed out the door.

I had been using an alarm
since she got sick two years before.

Every day after,
I'd been waking her with an injection
before catching the bus to school.

This was the only morning
she said she wanted to do it herself.
I was a teenager, happy to be off the hook.

The facts are simple.

This was the last time I saw her alive.
I was in US history as she pulled the trigger.

Every day I revisit that morning,
listening for an edge in her voice that wasn't there.
Looking for a pause, a quiver of her lip.

There was nothing special about goodbye.
There was no kiss. There was no hug.
She waved from the threshold.

Finding Her Face Down

The carton's straw
punctured the silver dot —
croaked a requiem
like the first atonal draw
on a student violin.
It splattered milk on my sweater
the way our carpet
caught pools of suicide.
Her withered breasts,
alreadied, unmuzzled,
lapped in the puddles
like hungry prunes
drinking on second thought.
Her finger's squeeze
blasted rapture to the ground,
like geese tumbling to our table
from the sky.
Serving plummet
on white bone plates
that buttoned the walnut seams
to stop the fall.
This meal will never quench
my thirst for milk.
It leaves me boring for breast
as I nurse the fabric clean.

Black Hole

police / paramedics
    g[love] the body
        she grew to hate

say it took ten minutes
    to form the puddle

i do not ask
    if she felt herself grow buoyant
    on sodden rug

they kneel / measure
    narrow diameter
        shore to shore

    say the mercy
was her weight
    compressing corpulent flesh
        to seal the breach
        dam the flow

backspatter bloods my photo
    her final view —
        iron on daughter's eyes
        tapioca fat [yell]owing walls

a black hole
drinks this galaxy
   thirsting

   like the hunger of body
  yearning for rest
swallowing lead for satiation

she crossed the event horizon
  gave herself to gravity

I wring my sponge
  watch the rosé water
   orbit faster and faster

spiraling down the drain

Flashback off Exit 74

In the gas station bathroom,
my heartbeat is the sound of dial tone —
so quick it's mistaken for a flatline. ~~Running~~
Humming in the red, through the after-splash
of a deer splitting, through tires plinking
gravel on the metal sign as they spin,
through the spit-soaked Goddamnits
splattered on the side view mirror. Alone,
with that vibrato in my chest, I'm chasing
my heartbeat down. At the faucet
my face is sink-splashed. Pale green
from the ice bone chill of water
winter-piped to my skin.
The fluorescent bulb is the speedbump I need.
Droplets falling from my chin
freeze mid-drip in its strobe. My arms
are stop motion staccato. Knuckles
cling garlic white to the porcelain rim
while my veins color up. Their glacier blue web
catches my pulse. Every loop and twist is a chicane,
begging my blood to slow.

Tangent Lines

There was no letter.
There were letters everywhere
inked in red. Splatter

confetti-bombing their bedroom
the day before Valentines.

A week later, I went back to school
needing a new calculator for trig.

Dad drove me to the mall,
handed me some paperbacks in a heart-shaped bag.

If you need a calculator so damned bad,
then return her presents and use that money.
I'll wait in the car.

I had no cash of my own.

Somewhere, two Dean Koontz books
meant for a dead woman are propped on a bedside table.

Every cosign and tangent I calculated
felt like a theft.

I Won't Tell You

I became that *thing*.
That girl lost one February,
who still showed up every day.
In the hallways. In your locker mirror.
That contagion walking. That
reminder, it could happen to you.
I became that *thing*
on the milk carton. A face
pleading to be found. The funeral
was a d[raw]n line between me
and not me. Her body [was]
ground to dust. My body kept living.
Or was reborn. Because afterwards [I was]
a story. The girl whose mother dies
is defined by nothing else. In her future,
only the past tense applies. *She had*
things lined up. She was applying
to university. Today, I'm still living
in history. When people ask,
I won't say it. Suicide
evokes pity. I've chosen silence
ever since the day my family
tried to monetize my grief.
Turned my shoulders toward
the scholarship committee and said
Tell them your story.

Autopsy Report: Between the Lines

second thoughts did not arise

There was no blood on her hands.
She had not pressed her palms
to the open wound.

cheek to floor

She did not kneel down, settle herself softly
on the carpet. She buckled hard
from sudden paralysis.

death was fast

The vena cava is the largest vein.
Ruptured, it gushed like a hose in her abdomen.
She lost consciousness quickly.

intent was clear

.38 lead wadcutter bullets
have a blunt nose, flush with the jacket.
Their flat faces are more damaging than a rounded tip.

a loose contact wound

She did not push the muzzle tightly into her belly,
wince as the cold of the steel penetrated her nightgown.
She was seeking comfort.

The Sin of Telling
(Not Showing)

The writer's group focused on loss.
I shared a poem about mom's suicide.
The other women spoke about miscarriage
spousal death. One man wrote of war.
Together, we faced cancer, Alzheimer's,
car accidents and amputation.

Have you tried first person?
This phrasing feels a little cliché.
The comments were constructive, supportive,
until they got to mine. *This is totally implausible!*
How could a woman get ahold of a gun?
You're asking too much here.

Too much of what?
The only reason you bring up suicide
is to get sympathy. You're burdening the reader.
The poem explored the stigma of suicide —
the multiple reasons why loved ones
stay silent.

A Mother's Shells

I use furniture to hold loss at bay—
shut drawers reserving her secrets for my future.

I'm tired of using anticipation
as a surrogate for resurrection.

It's time I pull the brass handle and return
her nightstand to timber.

Its track is dry. Hickory chafes into the air.
So many memories are built from the scent of wood.

I smell the rafters in the barn, see my mother holding a fallen nest.
One of my hair ribbons was woven among the twigs —

a single strand stopping disintegration.
There was no trace of the eggshells.

She said parent birds fly them away, hidden from predators.
A mother's instinct is to protect her young.

I think of this as I sort the contents of her drawer.
Pictures, pressed flowers returning to dust,

and tucked in the back corner — my milk teeth nestled in tissue,
roots still stained with my body.

Newton's Third Law

Stems bounce back,
fill my wake.

Flannel and wellies
carve my path through mayapples.
My forehead rests on the shovel's handle.

A hole is a simple thing.

An absence. An appetite scooped away. Plundered
by the spade. Fullness
in negative.

Like a halo of water
betrays the plunge of a stone through surface.
Then silence—

between heaving breaths.
Pouncing on the blade like fox on vole.
Boring into the marrow, I am
a woman splitting earth.
Raping and birthing
in parallel.

My arc of hands, my open palms,
squeak on the handle. Calloused skin
is a balm and a pock
in tandem.

Below the break in the canopy,
I plant this memorial tree, fill the space
between the elms.

The burlap peels away.
Roots dangle. Raw nerves,
seeking cover.

With the root ball seated in the wound,
this excavation is burial anew.

Out of Season

The window is a barrier
between my morning coffee and the outside world.

      I sit with my hands cupping a mug,
      looking right through.

Bird flight has become the bitter drive of hunger,
a dark *V* slicing white sky.

      I watch geese land in the field,
      rooting for the kernels that remain.

The tree line is a lavender haze —
frosty crowns reflecting the sunrise.

      Their bare limbs do nothing to stop the cold wind
      from scrubbing tractor-rippled ground.

It is November, and the soil is dry
lifting easily above the rows of cut stalks.

      My eyes linger on the nudity
      of earth and wood.

Bleak is the name we give to these weeks
between leaf and snow.

    After the harvest, I can see things plainly
    until summer covers it back up.

Natural light has faded even the flowers
printed on mom's old tablecloth.

    The fabric hanging over the shaded edge
    blooms out of season against my knee.

Acknowledgments

A special thank you to my husband Scott for bringing me endless rounds of coffee while I wrote, and to my friends Monica, Danita, Bonnie, Heidi, Marie-Louise, Sharon & Eric for all their encouragement and support.

Thanks to a whole crew of fellow writers who keep me fueled and energized and who always read early drafts in the dead of night: Andy, Jessica, Lorraine, Mark, Walter, Karen & Millie. You know who you are!

And to my mother, who gave me life.

I'm most grateful to the editors at the following journals where several of these works were originally published, sometimes in a different form.

Sky Island Journal: "Newton's Third Law" and "The Move"

Palette Poetry: "Rewind" (formerly published under the name "Escaping the Family Legacy")

The American Journal of Poetry: "Unzipped," "Autopsy Report: Between the Lines," "Genesis," "The Cost of our First House," and "She Said It"

The Front Porch Review: "Out of Season"

The Shore: "She Spoke with Urgency"

Crack the Spine: "Botany: A Side Effect of Treatment"

FRiGG: "Metamorphosis" (formerly published under the name "Mirror Images")

SOFTBLOW: "Finding Her Face Down"

After the Pause: "Black Hole"

Empty House Press: "A Mother's Shells"

About the Author

Lorrie Ness was born in Indiana and currently lives in Virginia with her husband and a menagerie of pets. She completed her doctorate in psychology from the University of Tennessee and her writing is deeply influenced by the complexities of human relationships and our connections to the natural world. When she is not writing, she can be found hiking, photographing insects, and playing in the dirt. This is her first collection and her previous works can be found in a variety of journals.

Flowstone Press, an imprint of Left Fork, publishes contemporary poetry collections and chapbooks. Our tastes are eclectic, but we'll lean toward the lyrical, psychological, environmental, cultural, and imagistic.

To learn more about Flowstone, to view our guidelines for submission, or to purchase one or more of our books, please visit **LeftForkBooks.com/Flowstone**

CPSIA information can be obtained
at www.ICGtesting.com
Printed in the USA
BVHW051605310721
613263BV00016B/1069